From My Soul to yours

Late Bloomer

Inspired by childhood dreams,
imagination, curiosity,
life experiences, trauma,
the need to heal,
the universe,
but mostly, by Love...

Content

Light......................7

Darkness............31

Cure....................53

Redemption......81

Love....................103

Light

The Ocean

I haven't been away for so long
I was craving some goodness for my soul
Hungry for this mystical trip,
I walked through the woods,
I stood on the edge of a cliff
With one last look at the view,
full of positive emotions,
I jumped into the ocean
Hoping, I would reach its depths
Hoping, we would connect,
temporarily form same part of dna
So I could gain great insight,
to all that's unknown
I wished to make friends with all of its life forms
I wanted to become a part of that world,
experience it all inside my curious soul
Private tour, just for me,
how naive...
Once I've seen it all,
once I knew it all,
it couldn't be unseen,
it couldn't be unknown
I was in Love
I was in such owe,
that ocean, became my eternal home

Magical compulsion

My need to write is buried deep between my bones
This itch to share, embedded in my very core
I am constantly breeding intimate words,
sharing with you all what's playing inside my soul

London

Living in this city,
how not to get inspired?
Everything is so mysterious,
nothing is transparent
It almost feels like some kind of time travel
One minute, I'm in the eighteen hundreds
In the next, in the twenty first century
I have lived here for so long
Yet, all I want is to explore
There is still so much to discover,
so much more to see,
so many corners to unravel
History of this place
infiltrates my inner self
I never feel lonely
I feel connected and homely
This attachment so deeply implanted,
almost as if we were mutually enchanted

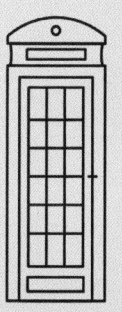

Wonders

Come, sit next to me
Allow me show you how great it can be
Open your heart to this possibility
Endless happiness and fulfilment
Just fall in love... with yourself
You'll see...

Clouds

Where do you hurry my dears?
Almost always on the move
What's your next destination?
It all seems like a mission
A calling of some sort
Something you can't resist
I hope you will get rewarded for your troubles
This unwavering faith and commitment
The universe
How uncanny

Dutchess Rose

Her fragrance is mesmerising
Her flower so feminising
Muskiness within her
makes me feel empowered
Thanks to her innocence
I feel wildly inspired
By the virtue of her woodiness
I am awakened,
almost transpired
My universe excitedly expanded
I am addicted,
my soul feels enchanted
She sends me to another dimension
Duchess Rose,
what a beautiful invention

 # Birds

I hope you don't mind me asking...
Are you comfortable up there?
Have you got everything you need?
Have you eaten today?
How far have you been?
Are you all alone in this world?
Have you got a place called home?
Is anyone waiting for you?
Am I making you tired?
Just one more thing, please
With all my heart I ask you
Come down and sing for me
Or just sing from up there
May your song tell me what you see
I bet it's pure magic

Awaken

It has begun
I've been asleep again,
now I'm awake
So so grateful
Another chance
Will is here again
Intention also turned up
Energy is on her way
All coming together now
I can see it all, from afar
In my mind, it is nearly touchable
My hand, guided by my imagination,
lifting up towards that light

La dolce far niente

Resting minds
Bodies relaxed
All troubles put aside
Nowhere to rush
Pleasant idleness
Our souls latest crush
La dolce far niente
The sweetness of doing nothing
So deserved in these current times

Human race

Lying in bed at night
looking through my bedroom window,
admiring all the stars...
How they come alive
This beautiful sky is making me wonder
about all of Us
Human race...still so much to do
Yet, I can't help to think
how far we've already come

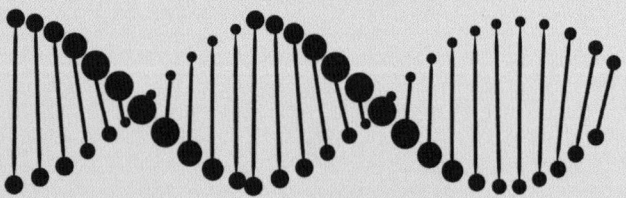

Community

How special...
Being part of community
Being recognised when visiting local cafes,
flower shops, parks
Having chats with your neighbours,
with the elders passing by,
with business owners, dog walkers
Being part of local involvement
Looking after the homeless
Having sense of belonging
Never feeling lonely
Supporting other human beings,
what a beautiful feeling...

Saviour

I am in the noise and in all the silence
In all Your dreams and whispers
Bringing light,
saving You from the darkness

Sister

Smiling so brightly,
shining incandescently
Like a touch of an angel,
she makes it all go away
I forget all my troubles,
my worries and upsets
Without any effort,
she keeps improving my mindset
Effortlessly bringing light to my soul
Her eyes full of warmth, admiration, console
She means so much to me,
more than whole world
My sister, my friend, my bundle of love

Colours of life

Never give up
Open your heart
Let in the light
Love someone
Fight for your dream life
Be courageous
Be brave
Be enough

Multiverse

In my virtual multiverse
I am Edith Piaf busking in Montmartre
Marie Curie enjoying the enlight
Sophia Loren in "Two Women„
Frida Kahlo expressing on linen
Ellen MacArthur sailing through
Cape of Good Hope
I am also just Me...
Uniquely bespoke

The Almighty

Angelic voice whispering inside my soul
"You are loved beyond possible
Magnitude of this love is beyond imaginable
Close your eyes,
feel the light
You have nothing to worry about
I wrapped you in invisible vail,
protecting your every cell
You are never alone,
it's impossible
We are collective,
You are part of me,
molecularly,
and I am The Almighty
To some known as The Universe
Just look inside or look up,
when you need me... that's where you'll find me,,

Ignition

When you feel good in your own skin
There is nothing you can't achieve
No mountain you can't climb
No peak you can not reach
All you need is a sprinkle of luck,
and just a touch of believe

Rainbow

Colourful rainbow on the sky
Parting gift, after days of rain
Sunshine is here now,
even though still a little shy,
somehow I know, it is here to stay

Space for The Light dancing inside Your soul...

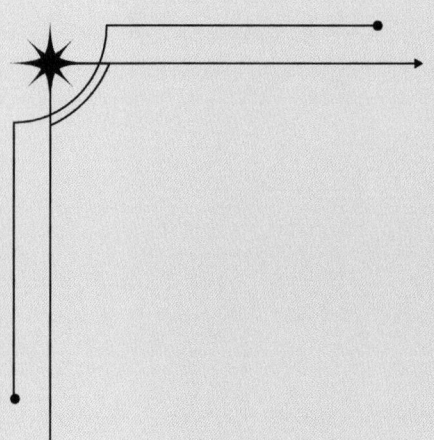
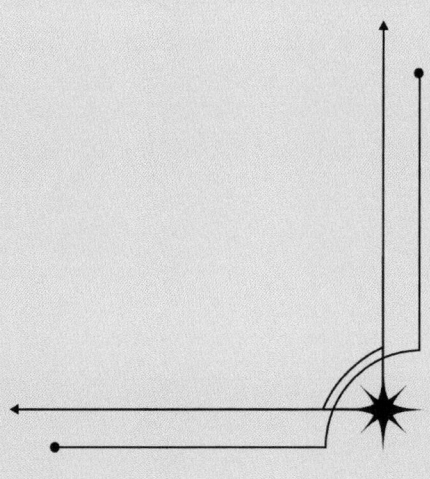

Space for The Light dancing inside Your soul...

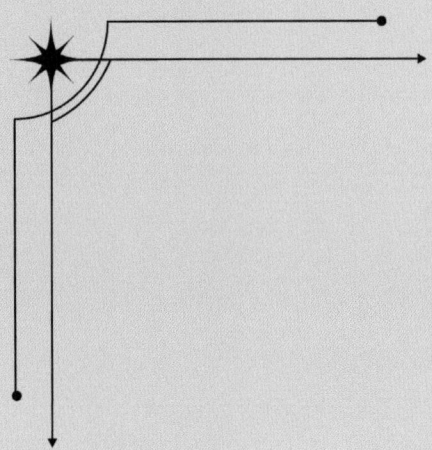
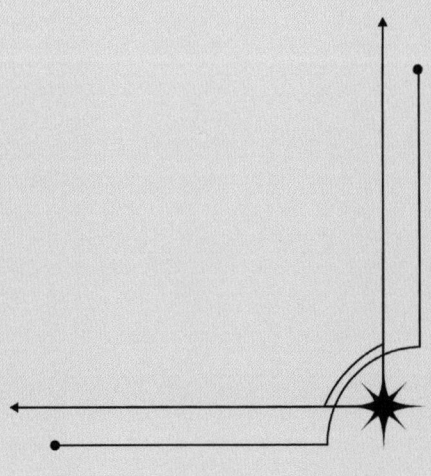

Space for The Light dancing inside Your soul...

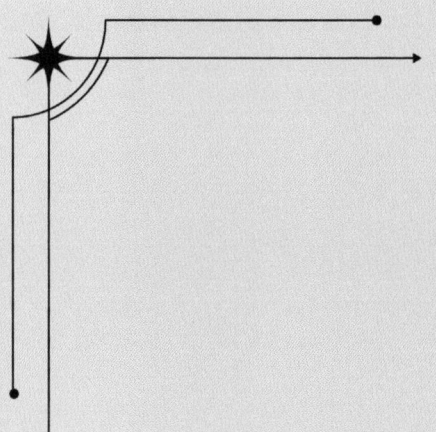
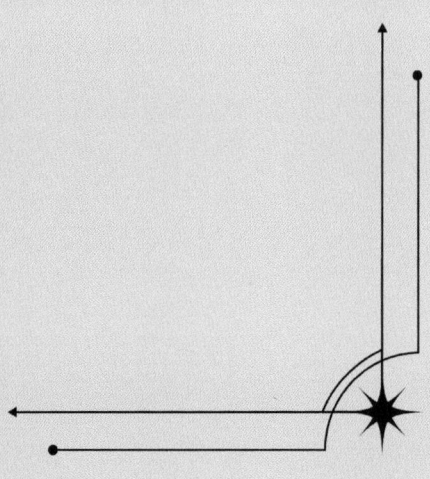

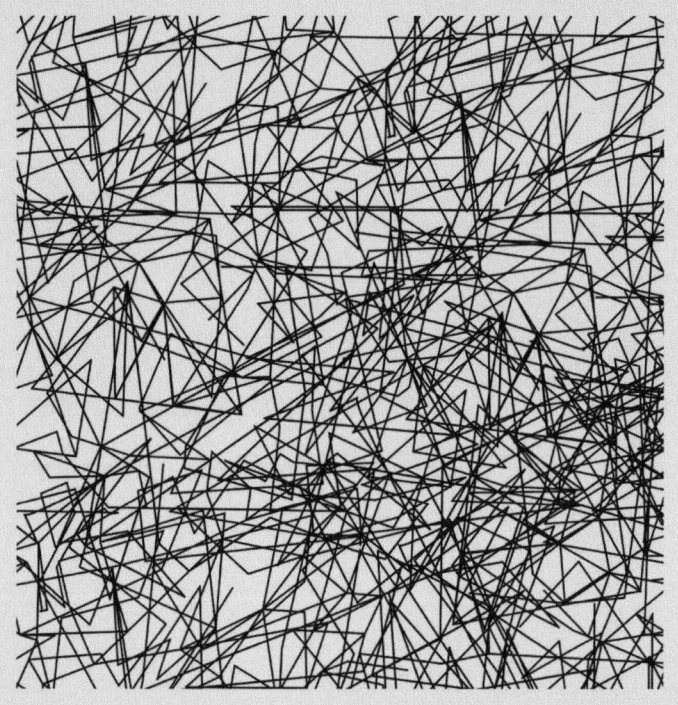

Darkness

Camouflage

Suffering heart, hiding under false facade
Emanating happiness,
pretending everything is fine
Quietly crying bloody tears,
slowly giving up

Mother

So many things to tell You
So many questions to ask
I often wonder,
will I ever get another chance
I don't know if to be angry
or to be sad
I'm confused with all this grief
eating me inside
So much time has passed,
never changed a thing
I still miss You so much
I really need another drink
It won't fix for long the way I feel
This temporary numbness,
it is my artificial heal

Kazik

Wooden slates, snowy trips
Wooly blanket
So I wouldn't feel cold...
You, tucking me in
With you being close,
I felt protected,
I felt untouchable
I loved playing our games, checkers, chess
I loved your delicious soups,
though, mostly made out of stolen goods
You never called me by my name,
always using lovingly nickname
You were my everything
I wished I only remembered all the love
Unfortunately, I remember it all
Devilish, tyrant of sorts
Than again, biggest heart of them all
Confusing to the little girl that I was
How was this possible?
So good to me, so evil to others
Somehow...
This never changed my love for you my dear father
People say love for a child is unconditional
I think with us, it worked both ways
It's been so long since you've been taken away,
but I still miss you like it was yesterday
I always feel the blues on your birthday
I've come to realise...
Loosing You, will never get any easier

Dreaming

I am up in the sky,
flying so high
Mingling with the stars,
chatting with the Moon,
having tea with Mars
Gazing at Jupiter in owe of its beauty and size
Thinking of using Saturn's rings as my personal slide
Looking at Venus trying to impress the Sun
Mercury investigating everything around
Neptune and Uranus giving me a bit of a cold welcome
Smirking from afar, I'm sure eventually both will warm up
Surrounded by my new friends
I am looking down and can't help to think
I don't want to go back, I don't want to wake up...

Armageddon

I hate you and I love you
I am grateful for you and I want to destroy you
I am thankful for everything you've done for me
I wish we never crossed paths for what you did to me
Because of you, I will never be who I was meant to be
You left me in this permanent horror I have to live in
You created this shattered, conflicted and sad human being
You killed all of my innocence
All greatness dreaming inside of me
One of the most precious gifts to this universe
is who I was destined to be
Instead, all that is left, is this gigantic nothingness
This experience destroyed me from within
My life was simply over, before it could begin

Personal hell

I gave you all...
I gave you my soul
A secret key to my inner garden
A private code to my hidden chamber
I allowed for you to fly over my skies
To walk on my Moon, see my Sun,
to reach for my Stars
Wasn't all that enough?
Finally, when your true self showed up
My whole galaxy collapsed just like that
It felt like true hell,
like I've met the devil,
and his only mission was my submission
It felt like I fell from the top of the Eiffel Tower
It felt like my darkest hour
Since then, I promised to my self
not to reach or climb this high, till the end of my days
You changed me, You took something from me back then
Maybe one day, I will be whole again
I will get back that piece of me
which I left all those years ago back there,
in my personal hell

Before

We met before, remember?
Such inner beauty
So pure, innocent
Impossible to forget
You were so young then
Do you remember?
All the love
All the dreams
All that goodness
Eagerness
Zest for life
We were so close back then
Today...I barely see you

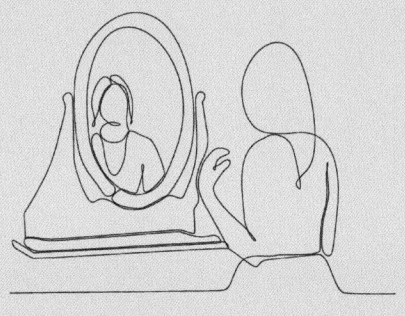

Blood sucker

Emotional leech,
attached to my already aching skin,
sucking out all of my blood
I'm sweating to say the least
What if there will be nothing left?
What if I cease to exist?
I'm so afraid
If I fail to act now,
soon enough...
there will be nothing left of the old me

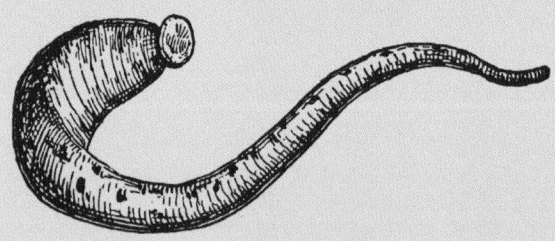

Scars

Hidden scars,
engaged in a never ending dance
Learning new routines,
wanting to survive
So keen to win this contest,
hardly ever giving up

Regret

I'm sorry for letting you down,
for making you sad
I ache for what I've done
I'm sorry for unfulfilling your needs
My shallow side got the better of me
I was selfish,
self-centred,
forgot how to act
I will get better,
I promise,
just let me have one more try
I need to see you happy,
joyful and full of life
One more chance,
that's all I ask
I know I can make it right

Unreplaceable

I look into her eyes and I see her pain
I see how much she is missing her
How much she is craving to see her face
Have another conversation
With a lot of admiration, seek another advice
Like always before, share her life
Her mother, her everything, her best friend
Gone way to soon, how unfair
This titanic love between the two of them
Mother to daughter, daughter to mother
As it happens a lot, with destiny at work,
both hearts have been shattered
I hope one day, in another realm,
this time forever, they will find each other again,
and their happiness will never end...

Cockroaches

We always meet at night,
when no one's watching
Causing havoc,
relinquishing all darkness
Night needs it,
it feeds on it,
black hole swallows it all without trace
Without Us,
night wouldn't be night

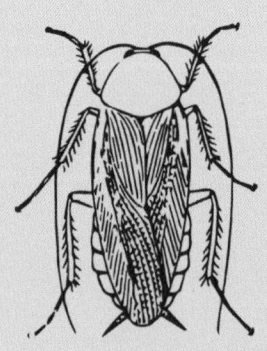

Missing

Where are you?
I'm worried,
please show yourself to me...
Say something, whisper in my ear, do anything...
I've lost sight of you and I don't know where could you be
I can't find you anywhere
and it's time to get back on that stage
It's time for us to act, if you are not here...
how will the audience react?
They all will be shattered,
especially Mrs Soul and Mr Heart
You only really have one true choice here,
eventually, you must join me, you must show up...

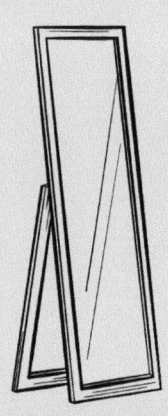

Storm

Tornado passed through me
leaving almost everything destroyed
Strong winds still blowing
inside my damaged core
Now, huge fire is trying to burn it all
I can feel my end is near,
what a bad way to go

Disaster

Moon fell down and can not be found
Sun blew out, now, unable to shine
Stars no longer capable to light up the sky
Darkness took over, swallowing everything around

Zombies in the woods

Constantly indulging in self gratification,
adopting desires of others as our own
on deeper level knowing this is so wrong,
we just can't stop
Consequently, we forget who we once were
Finding ourselves on this road to nowhere
Depleted, stripped of our core values
Like Zombies in the woods,
we shallowly travel through this life of ours

Space for The Darkness troubling Your soul...

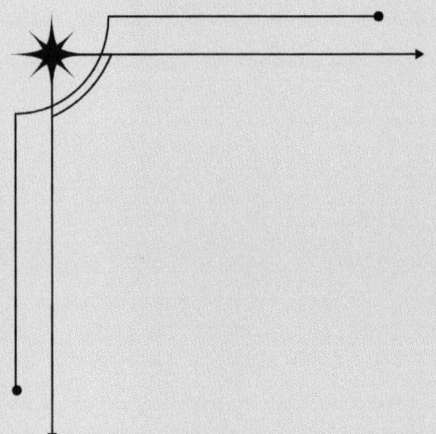
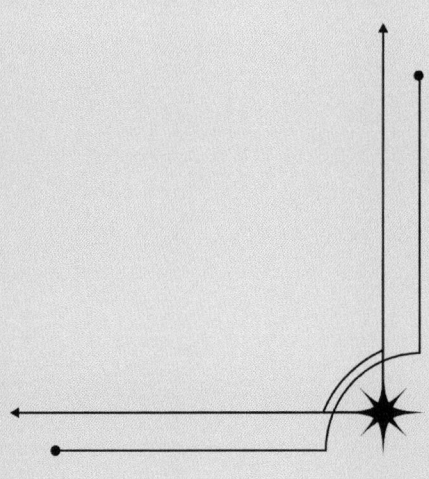

Space for The Darkness troubling Your soul...

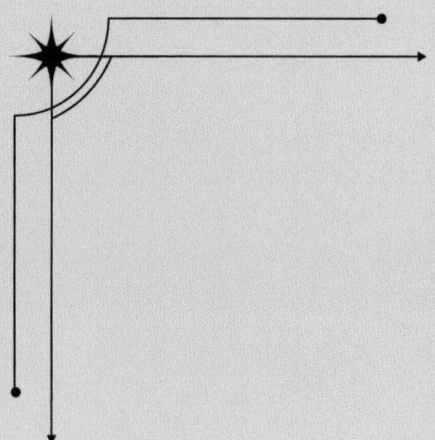
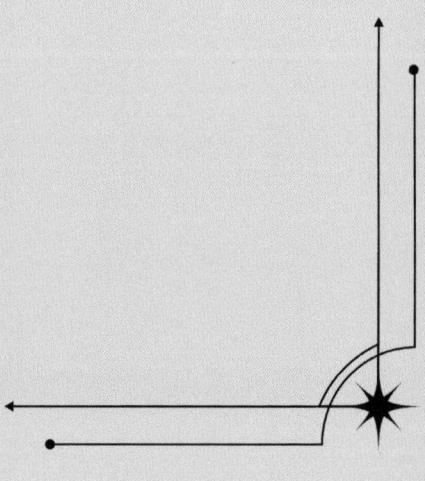

Space for The Darkness troubling Your soul...

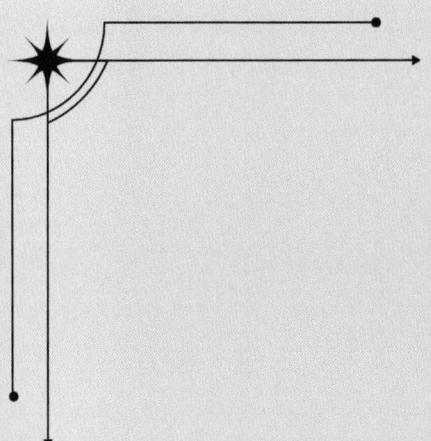
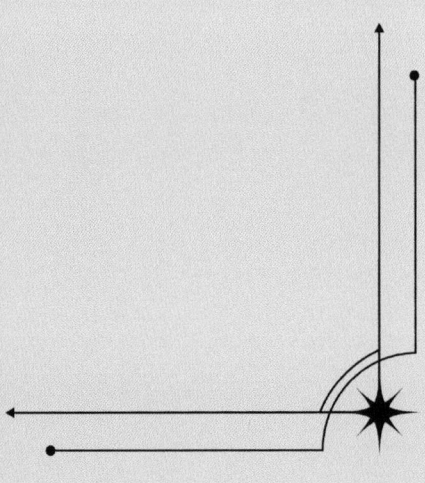

Cure

Restless mind

Curious wind rustles inside my soul
Restless mind itching my very core
My hungry heart on a lookout for something more...

Midnight sky

Every time I look at you...
you amaze me,
and I looked at you a thousand times by now,
if not more...
Divine beauty, mysterious, unreachable,
shining upon us...
Every time I look at you...
I feel you inside me, a doorway within,
to a such magical place
Everything is possible
Thank you, truly
I couldn't do without you
Without all your gifts
And they say nothing is for free
Yet, you just keep on giving...

Raven

Gazing at me he stopped ever so briefly
Before flying away, he touched my soul,
intensely and deeply
For in this mystical moment, his black eyes told me a story
Story of a girl, girl in her glory
From that day, it's like he is always there
Sitting on my shoulder, making sure I'm ok
My beautiful Raven, I wish I could return the favour
I truly hope, one day we will meet again
This time, I will make you whole,
like you made me that day

Paree Paree

Paree Paree...
I can hardly find any words to describe
how you make me feel
Montmartre, medicine for my soul
Just being here makes me feel whole

Paree Paree...
Every time we meet,
beauty is all I see
I can't contain myself around you
It's pure magic what you do to me

Paree Paree...
City of love they say
I am in love with you to such depth
Until my last day,
until my last breath

Montmartre

It's where I belong,
where my artistic soul is at home
Nowhere else do I feel more whole,
elated to my core
It's hard to describe this feeling
This place, connected to my entire being
Entwined, with me and my way of thinking
Guiding my inner goddess,
my entire creative progress
This place is always with me
Montmartre...
Where my soul was born,
where my being awoke
Where I was shown, I could be so much more
Where I remembered, who I truly was...

April

Blooming flowers all around,
sun smiling at me from the sky,
feeling of calm
I'm looking around
listening to the whistling trees
Only one thought comes to mind,
what a bliss...

Sunny meadows

I love summers
Soaking up the sun,
smelling all the flowers
I love lying in the grass,
listening to the birds,
drinking wine,
dreaming,
gently cradled by the meadow
I truly love that feeling
All of this is so organic to me
In those moments,
there is no other place I would rather be

Games

I feel your teeth breaking my skin
I feel your claws digging into me
You pounce on me so quick, so focused to win
I know you're only playing
No worries, soon enough, you will be obeying

Werewolf diaries

Nightfall called my name
Pulling me closer it whispered...
"Don't worry, all Your secrets are safe
Don't be shy, go and be free
No judgement here, it is just You and Me
Under my wings...
You can thrive until dawn
Blossom in Your full form
Transcend inside Your soul„

The beach

Sound of the waves
Soft breeze gently blows in my face
Eyes closed
Blissful notes
The sun penetrating me inside out
My bare feet cooling down buried in wet sand
There is something so special in this simple moment
Some kind of higher power involvement
I forget all my torments
My whole being is almost transported
State of my consciousness somehow altered
No past and no future
No yesterday and no tomorrow
Just here and now
Entirely connected
The sun, sea, sand, wind and I

Ambleside

My magical peaks...
You put my being into such bliss
Enchanted lakes...
Thank you for our joyful dance
I love when we are singing soulful notes together
Telling stories, promising loyalty to each other, now and forever
Only you know how to mend my broken wings
Bringing wisdom, clarity, needed tears
Enabling me to fly again
Connecting me with my holy grail

Dawn at the lakes

Wooden chair on the pier
Me...cross legged with a cup of coffee in one hand
Looking at mystical fog hovering above the lake
Forest waking up just behind
Pine, releasing it's essence everywhere around
Bringing bliss, mending my broken mind

Winter blues

Snowy hills
Crispy steps
Frozen lakes
I'm so amazed

Waiting for Spring

I love your essence
So happy you will bless us with your presence,
making life so much easier
Everything around colourful, sunny, pleasant
Once again, you will charge up our energy levels
Cycling trips
Park meetings
Grass sittings
Bench kisses
Soul whispers
Can't wait for you
I am so glad you will be here so soon

Precious gifts

Sound of the waves, brown noise for my veins
Mountains and their tracks, aspirin for my blood
Rivers and lakes, wash away my pain
Ice and cold, soap for my soul
Sun and warmth, battery for it all
Trees, my greatest allies
Mycelium, answer to all of my sorrows
What an undeniable connection
Genesis of all creation

Friendship

Friendship, how to define it?
Well, let me tell you what I know about it
I know this guy, friend of a friend
We...haven't actually met
He lives there, me here
Somehow, it doesn't mean a thing
Like some kind of a string, there is this magical bond,
connecting us both
Through music and vibration, mutual energy and adoration
For someone he barely knows, he takes time out of his day
He creates this beautiful moment, for someone so far away
He send me birthday wishes
With those, there is also a song
Not just any song and sang so beautifully,
with such intention,
when you're listening to it, there goes all your attention
All else fades into oblivion
Suddenly...
You are wrapped in this love, truth and care,
by someone you don't even know you that well
And it might seem like nothing,
just some wishes with a song
True meaning here is how, and who from...

Arai

If I haven't met you,
where would I be?
In emotional prison,
forgetting all about me
I owe you so much,
there's no words to describe,
how grateful I am,
to have you as a friend
You gave me that chance,
new life, and so much more
Confidence to thrive,
to reach for it all
But life is life
and right now you're so far
I hope you know, that for the rest of my time
Your name is engraved in capital letters,
in the depths of my heart

Sasha

My sweet boy...
You give me so much joy
Every time I look at you
all I see is Love,
and yes,
I see how you look at me
I can read you so easily
I see your comfort,
I see your frustration,
I see how you plead for my attention
and I weep...
Time is not on my side
I wish I could give it all

Companion

Longing for wilderness,
longing for pray
That raw taste,
fresh blood,
satisfaction and pride
Missing all that excitement
I might be choking,
I need air
"Please, release me,
I promise, I will see you again,,
"Ok,, she said
"Wait...
hold up...
I'm scared,
I don't think I can make it
I think I'll stay here a while
longer,
It's kind of cosy here anyway,,

The Moon

We love the Sun,
but out Sun can also harm
We love all other Stars,
but all other Stars as cherished as they are,
can devastate when falling down
What about the Moon?
It is merely an object, not a star or a planet
We love it, but can it be as damaging as the others?
Merely an object? Damaging you say?
This beautiful mysterious glowing display?
Moon could never cause any distress
For Moon my dear is The Almighty Goddess
If you don't believe me, ask The Universe
Then look inside your soul and true answer will emerge...

Life

Magic
Light
Happiness
Contentment
Pleasure
Satisfaction
Pain
Sorrow
Sadness
Anger
Regret
I welcome You all

Freedom

I've realised something today...
Life is too short to dwell on mistakes
Too unpredictable, to waste even one day,
wondering...
What's gone wrong in the past?
Was there another way?
From now on, I will enjoy each and every day,
by being fully present here and now,
treating every moment as my last...

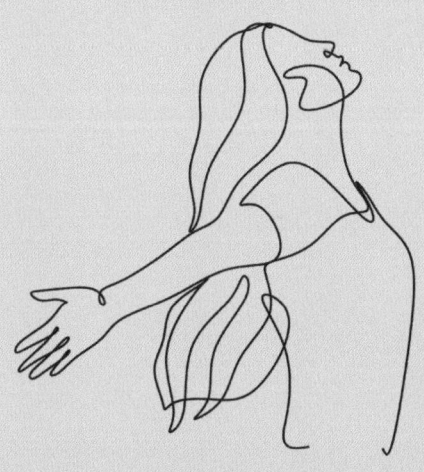

Space for The Cure healing Your soul...

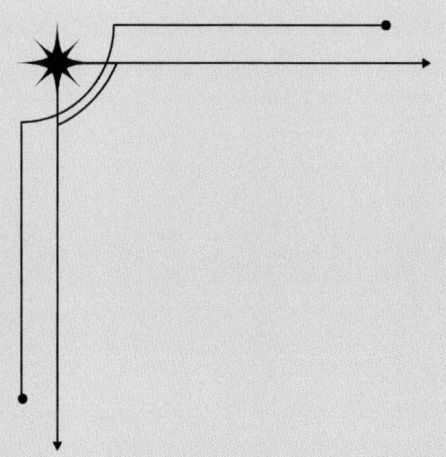
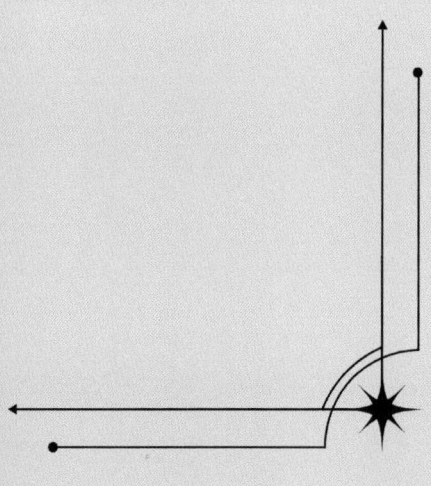

Space for The Cure healing Your soul...

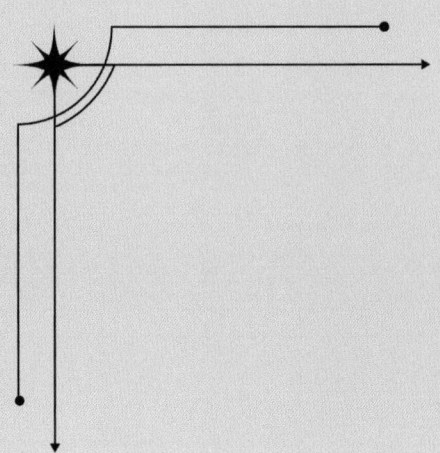
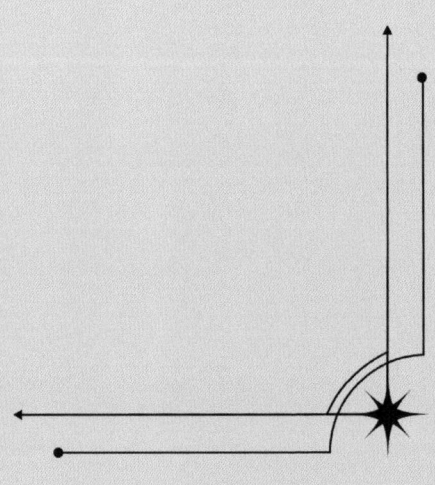

Space for The Cure healing Your soul...

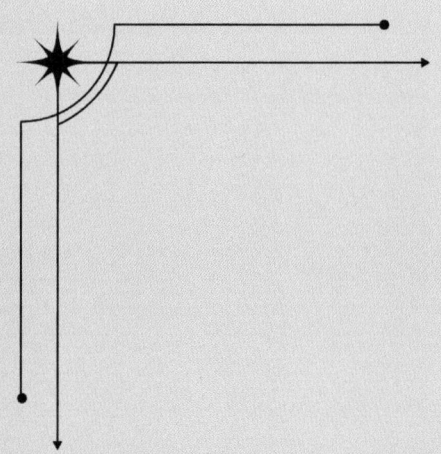
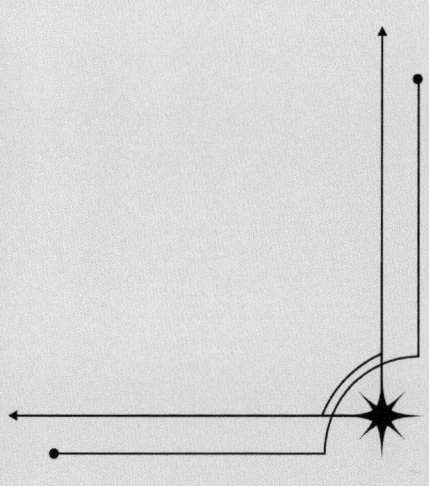

Redemption

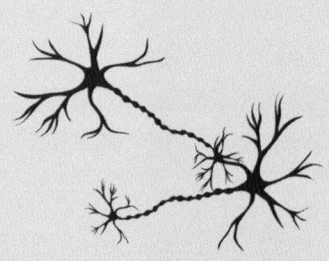

Us

Strong
Yet, so fragile
Innocent
Yet, so guilty
Beautiful
Yet, so ugly
Smart
Yet, so mindless
Generous
Yet, so parsimonious
Warm
Yet, so cold
Why may I ask?
No... no need to ask
It is all so clear...

Over overload

I thought it was over
Blood was taking over
I was expecting to fall over
But weakness never came
My genius brain knew how to play this game
Once again, I was saved

Bare

My vulnerable side on the surface of my heart,
acting as distraction from my truest path
With clarity absent from my fragile mind,
I've been feeling lost, for the longest time
I can't be here in this form, just trying to survive
I'm searching deep inside, for the power to ignite
Time after time, refusing to give up,
fighting to fulfil my destiny, as written in the stars...

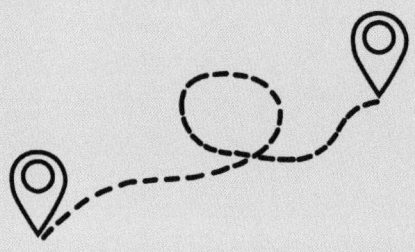

Contradictions

My soul seem to be drowning
Contradictions in my core are astounding
Will it end in my own demise?
Or is this paradox a saviour in disguise?

Resistance

Resistance is real
How can we win?
Distractions run high,
hopelessness all around
We are trying so hard,
to hack our absent minds
We hate this weakness in our fabrics,
those massive holes inside our souls,
those aliens infiltrating our thoughts
Enemies inside our walls,
broken chips inside our troubled brains,
those faulty veins
Dear Universe...
We can't accept this poisonous submission,
We have to get on with our life's missions
We need to manifest our visions
Please, blow some magic our way
Please, send your troops inside our heads
Unleash your greatest warriors
We will fight this fight united
We already feel ignited
It's possible!
Let's go

Holy Grail

Leave the outside world
Dive deep inside your soul
Meet the real you
Discover your truth
Light up your inner fire
Find your desires
Uncover your life's meaning
Align with your being
Be whole
and just be that,
nothing more
You can finally exhale
Welcome to your Holy Grail

Banana

I remember that taste like it was yesterday
It made me feel so good
One bite was enough,
to put me in this magical mood
It left me desperate for more
Than again, lack of all things,
maybe that's all what it was
Back then, it was like food from The Gods
What an illusion...
Available everywhere today,
it doesn't taste the same
If you have one just like it,
next day, you forget all about it
It's almost as if...
Lack of desperation removes the need for memorisation
So precious, this humbling lesson
A moral compass to avoid any obsessions
I might have everything, but perspective is all
Even a cup of coffee brings me a lot of joy
I always feel so alive
Dear me...
How I appreciate every smallest thing in this beautiful life...

Crossroads

Standing at the crossroads,
feeling like a lost cause
With a bit of luck,
a tiny guidance from the stars,
blow of whisper from natures arms,
I will choose it right,
finding myself on the right path,
mending my broken mind,
piecing in all missing parts...

Surprise

If only I could show you
what hides inside of this beautiful tree,
what lies in the depts of this majestic sea
Unexpectedly, you would fall in love,
Instantly, inherently...

Search

My pieces scattered all over the globe
Is my heart irreversibly torn?
Am I nothing more than a broken soul?
So far gone, so lost
I might disappear, how did I get here?
What now? Is that all?
Is that all that's left of me?
Surely it can't be...
What would it take? What would I need?
To feel like myself , to feel whole again,
to put all the puzzles back in their place
Furthermore,
where would I find all the strength?
to lift my self back up, to face what's messed up,
to act in different ways, to not be afraid
I guess I have no choice, I have to try
No one else will come to my rescue
I am my only chance
Only I can bring myself back to life

Reflections

It's probably the age I am in...
Causing me to reevaluate everything
Who I'm friends with,
what's important to me,
what I really want to achieve
Throwing away all that is borrowed,
all foreign follows,
all that resonates hollow
It's really hard to swallow...
How much time I've lost trying to please,
putting everyone else at ease
In the process of it all,
completely forgetting who I was
Neglecting all my desires and needs,
alienating all my believes
I truly hope I have enough time left here,
to live this life the way I want to live
I hope I've got enough courage now,
to experience it as a true version of me

Chance

I saw you staring at me,
You looked right into my eyes
But, it wasn't my time
That day, The Universe was on my side
I got a second chance
Chance to live my life,
to make things right,
to experience it all from a different frame of mind

Rescue

Gentle waves in my headspace,
waking up my neuro essence
Mending my broken connections
Working on all needed corrections
Rescuing my absent mind
I feel energised, somehow refined,
absolutely ready for that one final fight

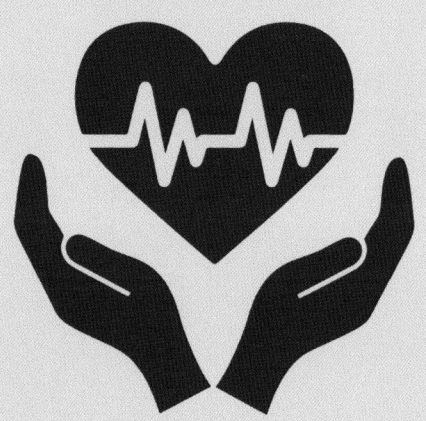

The Secret

Close your eyes, be present, here and now
Clear your mind, listen deeply to your beautiful heart
There, all answer can be found
Because the heart never lies
Only then, you can find yourself on your truest path...

Destiny

I've begun healing in all the places
Took me long enough, but here I am once again,
hungry, curious, restless
Extremely grateful, loving this moment in time
Joyously, bringing my old self back to life
My destiny awaits, well... here I come...

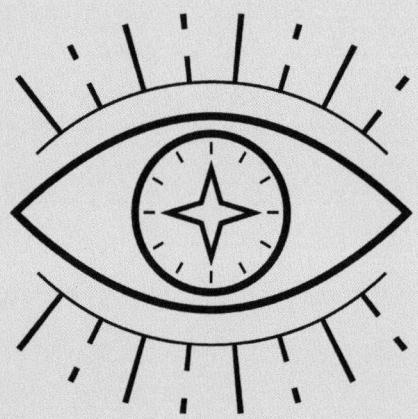

Truth to be told

We are fighting with all that we've got,
not to fall into a deep hole,
not to trip on a broken stone
We are trying to protect it all
But sometimes exactly what we need, is to dig underneath
To trip, to fall
To leave our comfort zone
To feel pain so unknown...
Only then we arrive at this door
„Please step in...on the other side is all that you want"

Shining star

Allow me to ask...
Why haven't you tried?
I wonder if maybe...
You were too shy
You felt intimidated,
immensely frustrated,
not up to the task
It was too hard every morning to even get up
Unreachable dreams...
stashed away in the furthest corner of your fragile mind,
forgotten about, now, smothered in thick dust
I assure you, not everything is lost,
the day will come...
When you are strong enough and ready to act,
when you are truly confident and calm,
sure of yourself and all of your choices
When everything you imagined and strived for combined,
becomes your reality and you start to shine
like the brightest star in the midnight sky
When you feel like you are on top of the world,
whatever this means in the depths of your soul...

Space for The Redemption saving Your soul...

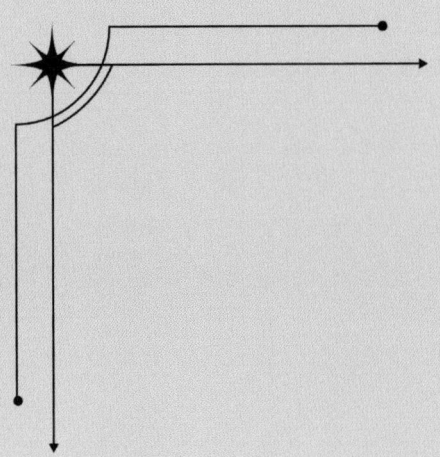
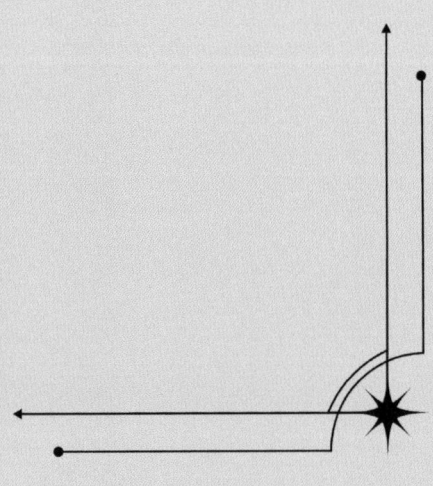

Space for The Redemption saving Your soul...

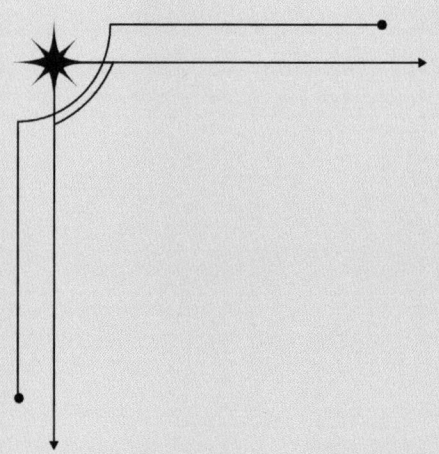
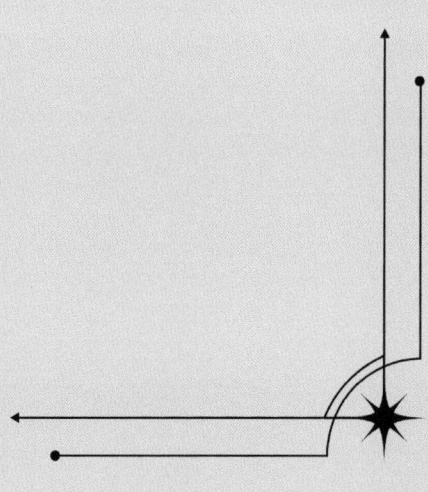

Love

River Nile

We will go to river Nile,
so we can board an ancient ship
No one else,
Just You and Me
We will watch the sun go down,
breathlessly
When the night will come,
guided by the midnight sky,
We will sail under Egyptian stars
Endlessly,
blissfully,
towards eternal ecstasy

If...

If our lips were to finally meet...
We would be lost forever...
gone...eternally

Electric love

Electricity runs through me,
dancing inside my veins
Like cosmic dust, romancing with my brain
Tickling my heart and soul,
making me fall in love
I am now shining brighter than
the Moon and the Sun,
brighter than all the Stars
Brighter, than anything in the skies…

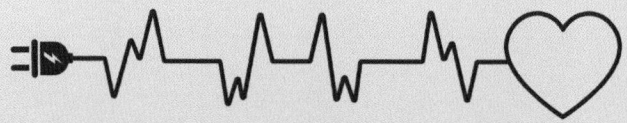

Hostile takeover

I want to devour your heart
Make home inside your soul
Run in every vein
Be inside your brain
Taking over your mind
Making you eternally mine

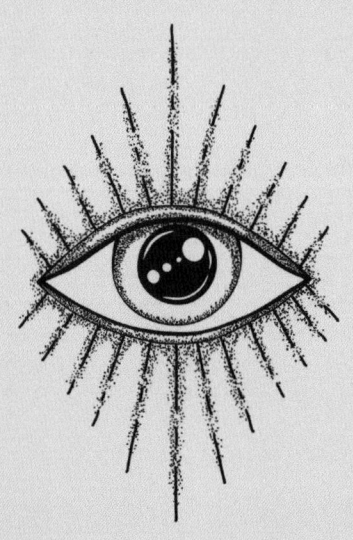

Brown Eyes

A vivid vision of You and Me
Consumed, captivated
Totally absorbed
I breathe You in my dreams...

A Kiss

No longer out of reach,
our lips finally meet
Tips of our tongues
warming up,
now in full mode...
enjoying this never ending dance

A wish...

I wish I could tell you how I really feel
How deeply your soul made roots inside of me
I only ever had one simple dream,
to take you with me on this special trip
This magical city...just You and Me
Enjoying each other, how great would it be
But you are hers and I am his, so this is it
This beautiful dream... will never be real

A dream

Your eyes piercing through me,
I'm shaking inside, I can't breathe
I can feel your warm breath on my trembling lips
My whole being is begging for that long awaited kiss
Your masculine arms pulling me closer,
I've lost all composure
Your warm hand sliding down my back,
brushing against my skin,
burning like the sun...
Your lips now resting on mine,
I'm loosing my mind
Sudden voice inside my head
"It's time to wake up, new day ahead,,
"No no no Dear Nyx
I don't want to end this dream
I want to stay asleep
Please, don't let me wake up
Let this be a never ending night,,

The Sun

When you are gone from the horizon...
My goodness, I feel so lost without you
This separation makes me feel so weak,
I can barely stand up or breathe,
I can't even think
I am hiding in my shell,
fighting for survival
All of my cells, trying to preserve all I have left
My whole being is shutting down,
I think I will die, but not soon enough
Unless...
I could set my eyes on you again,
feel your sweet embrace one last time,
once more, taste your breath
That would be worth this slow painful death

Desire

Fire inside of you is burning like the sun
You are trying to hide it, trying to deny
But the way you look at me,
It is all in your eyes...

Baia Mare

My soul broken in half
There is no other way,
I must say goodbye
Oh! my aching heart,
without him...
nothing will make sense,
nothing will suffice...

Without You

Without you...
I would disappear into oblivion
My soul would fall into a deepest hole,
my mind simply could not survive
With you by my side my love,
I can be anyone I want,
I can do it all,
I can save the world

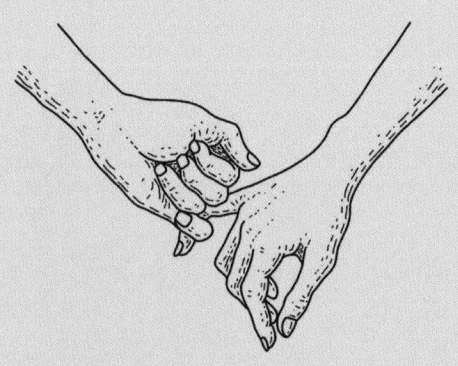

Army of Stars

My life was already a lot,
still, I was doing ok, I thought I forgot
Unexpectedly, I got a whiff of you, and that's all it took,
to fall in love anew,
to dismiss all reason
Once again, my heart was imprisoned
My guts were twisting inside,
I was asking myself, what now? how will I survive?
Then I remembered to look at the sky...
In that one simple moment, I've realised I would be fine
I was protected this time around...
I had a whole army of stars, ready, by my side...

Déjà vu

It happened again...
Electrical charge rushed through our veins,
living our minds astray
With this magnetic force at large,
our beings exploding inside,
we gave in, engaging in this familiar dance...
Looking at each other in this very moment we realised,
this thing between us...whatever it was..
no longer could be denied...

Sweet embrace

Sweet embrace of your heart sent me into epic meltdown
All my barriers have been crushed
Enchanted by your love,
I was reaching for the stars
Cosmically charged up,
seeing the whole Universe through us,
I knew right then...
I would never ever give you up

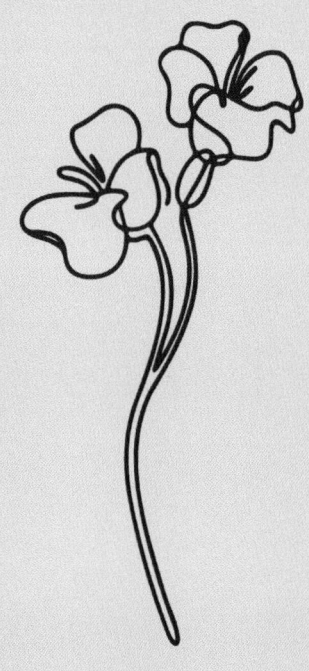

Virtual love

It's crystal clear,
we are in love and it's real
Our beings eternally entwined,
moving through space and time
Breathing same air,
always together,
imagining our life...
Making love
Talking, reading, travelling
Experiencing new things,
sharing and crying,
joking and laughing
Learning from each other,
smiling looking at one another
All so effortless,
as if written in the stars,
this virtual love out of Mars
How sad, that we are so shy..
How sad, this only happens in our hearts and minds
In reality, maybe one day, maybe some time
Most probably...in another life

Immersion

This possibility...so dreamy,
once in a lifetime really
Thoughts, hot and steamy,
fearing close proximity
Eyes meeting, stomachs keep turning,
it feels like we're burning
This mutual attraction,
internal combustion,
atomic explosion
Unshakeable magnetic pull,
beautifully real and pure
Runs deeper than any ocean
Whole carousel of intense emotions...
Why follow society rules?
Why act against our truth?
Why engage in any reflection?
Let's live and immerse in this magical connection!

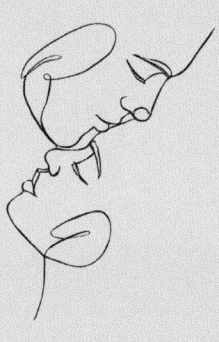

What could we be

You are intoxicating,
I can't stop thinking of you
It's all so overwhelming,
my soul feels abused
I can't help to think,
what could we be?
A thunder, a storm,
a force so unknown
We could conquer galaxies,
destroy all black holes
Discover new worlds,
create one of our own
If you destroy my defences,
possibilities are endless...

Concert of hearts

How powerful,
those musical endeavours
Sending us to the other side,
allowing exploration of our hearts
Giving insight, to our souls and minds
This road to discovery,
this magical trip,
led us to believe,
We could be anything...
Without any worries,
stepping into unknown territory,
we are free diving
Hoping for the best,
hoping it will last,
win, game of chance
So we can stay as we are,
for the rest of all time...

Mutual vibration

Music...
Dance floor...
Against all odds,
unable to resist,
they approach each other,
both knowing, it's what they need
To connect, to forget
To love, to live
It's electric, it's magnetic, it's eternal...

Selfless love

I need you...
I need you to be able to live,
to be willing to breathe,
wanting to exist
Yet, all I can think of is...
How unfair to you my dear,
to feel that kind of pressure,
if you ever wanted to leave...
My love for you, runs deeper than this
To set you free,
I would simply do anything...

Dilemmas of a broken heart

Although we don't want to admit,
we love each other more than a bit
As beautiful as it could be,
this love is out of reach
Guided by social rules,
fighting impurities,
torn by insecurities,
we're both denying this feeling
Thinking, this is the right way to act
It can't ruin anything,
it won't harm anyone but us
Stuck in this emotional jail,
we can't stop vividly dream about each other,
every night and every day

On the streets of Paris

I constantly see you in my dreams
One of them like blockbuster in theaters,
playing most nights on repeat
Me and You...
on the streets of Paris...
Indulging in its architectural beauty
Experiencing what's rightfully ours
Drinking fine wine, conversing, laughing
Enjoying our togetherness in a hotel room
Giving into this love and this enormous
magnetic connection
Completely swamped in mutual magic
This only being a dream...
So melancholically tragic

Shallow

Meat on the bone is what I'm looking for
Round hips, flat stomach
Full lips, rosy cheeks
No matter what's to say,
no matter the mind
As long as my eyes are satisfied

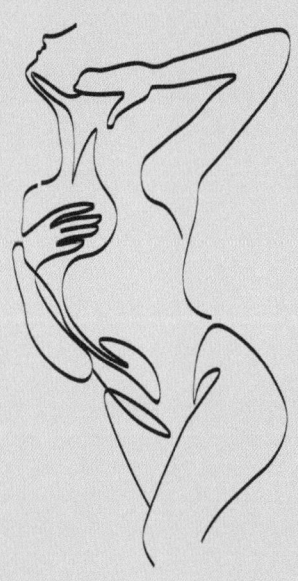

May

Spring fever
I'm a true believer
Natures love potion, hormonal explosion
Mind like confetti, feeling so sweaty
Emotional high, I'm no longer shy
Sex and romance, romance and sex,
playing on repeat inside my poor head
All those desires,
I feel like I'm on fire
This happens every year,
right on cue...in May

Twin soul

Craving to taste your blood,
couldn't wait for that first bite
So much insight...
My oh my, this is so familiar
Soul's secrets, heart's regrets, desires and dreams
How could I have missed it?
How could I not see?
My Twin Soul...
now out of darkness,
I am pining for you like never before

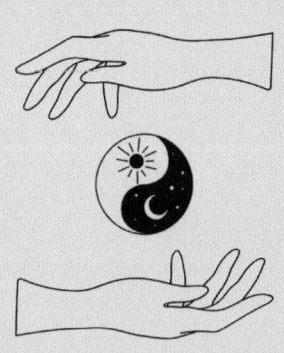

Whisper

Our minds alike,
our souls aligned
We are nothing more than friends,
it's a lot, it should be enough
Still, why do I constantly hear
The Universe whisper in my ear
"What a shame..You should be so much more
than that....,,

Beautiful mess

Let me take you where you've never been before
New highs, new lows
Allow me to test your boundaries
I am bound to put some life into your arteries
Now we are both is this crazy bubble
We only live once, let's get into some trouble...

Falling in love

Inside my stomach, uncertainty aura
Army of butterflies taking over
Mash potato inside my head
My brain, like a wreck from a head on crash with a speeding train
In my heart, soul and every vein,
nothing but lightning and torrential rain
Pain in disguise
Yet, I feel extremely alive...

All there is

You are making home inside my heart and soul
Growing roots inside of me,
like cordyceps taking over all I used to be
Making me a slave to this way I feel
I can't fight it, I am loosing my feet
Now all I can think about is you and that's it
It's like all other things in life ceased to exist
I am in love with you and that's all that there is
Whole Universe disappeared and I don't know where it now is
You is all I can see, all I can feel, all I can be
and the worst part is...
I love how it feels

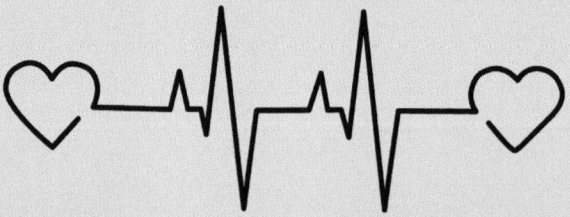

Star gazing

When I met you,
you surprised me in such different ways
Oh baby! I thought me and you would be together for many years
But time validates, looks through the cracks
You were not who you said you was
and it tore us apart
I often meet you in my lucid dreams,
but dreams are not real, and sometimes that kills
We were not meant to be, still, what wouldn't I give
for one more moment, one fantasy,
to become magically real
A sky full of stars,
field on a rise,
blanket on the grass
This one last time,
You and Me,
what a night would it be...

My sweet sweet Valentine

For a long time
I've been trying to deny,
how much I adore you,
how much I want you,
how I crave your lips,
how I dream about that one kiss
Every time I see you,
I'm trying to hide,
how my body reacts,
my pupils enlarge,
my fluids align
My secret crush...
Hidden from you... my sweet sweet Valentine

You and Me

My sweet darling...
We've been together for so long,
so many years have past, I've lost count
Our love for each other only grows stronger,
pulling us towards one another
We've never lost sight of how special this is
How beautiful, pure, innocent,
like this white feather flying in the wind
Sometimes, I look at you and I can't help to think,
how lucky we are to still have all of this
This love, this passion, desire and admiration
Need to be together, hating all separation
Sharing and caring, to mention few of so many
Hunny, this glue between us...not from this world
Me and You baby... we rule...we rule it all

Lost in the desert

One of a kind, this magical night
You and I, under the desert sky
Nothing ever felt as terrifying,
deeper or more beautiful,
than this moment in time

Elated hearts

Summer skies
Butterflies
Elated hearts
Intoxicated minds
Loved up eyes
Feeling of being alive
Someone to adore
Unknown soul to explore
Moments worth living for

Lovers

Lost in your eyes,
I'm reading what's in your mind
My warm hand on your chest,
feeling what's in your heart
Now I need you to see,
what's hiding in my mind
Put your hand on my chest,
feel what's in my heart
Don't be scared of what you'll find,
with our souls so eager to align...
let's embrace it,
let's bring this magic to life!
It's time...

Barcelona

Me and You
It was love at first sight
The way we connected...
It blew my mind
Almost destroyed my fragile heart
It filled my soul with such enlight
I am simply bound to You for the rest of my life

Where from...

Love, where does it come from?
Her principles mysteriously engraved in our core
Maybe it comes from the heart?
Maybe from the soul?
Maybe from them both?
It doesn't even matter
What matters is that it is still here
Connecting Us all
Making our lives worth living for...

Space for The Love transcending Your soul...

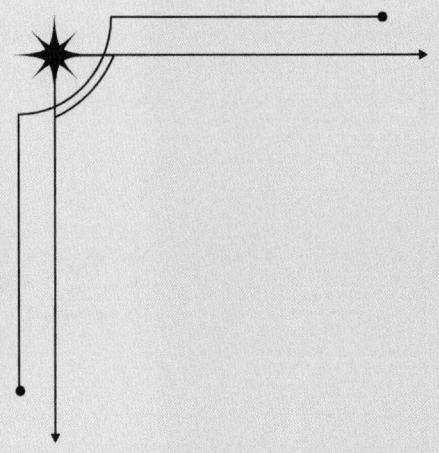
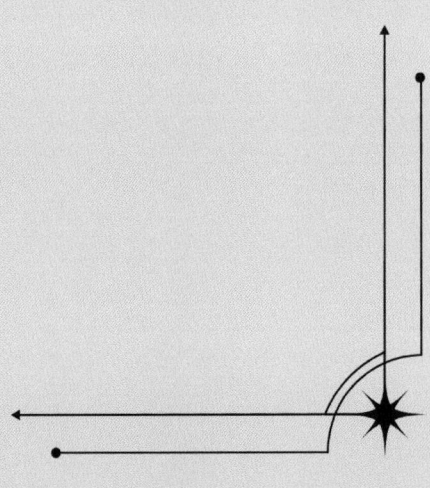

Space for The Love transcending Your soul...

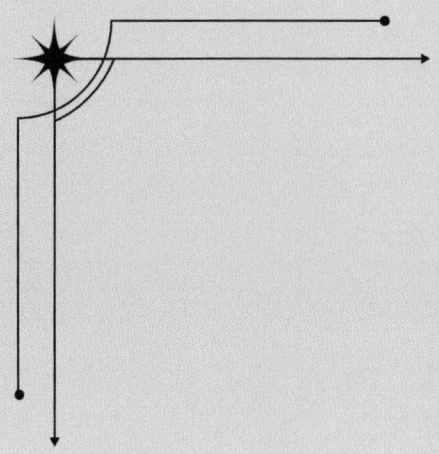

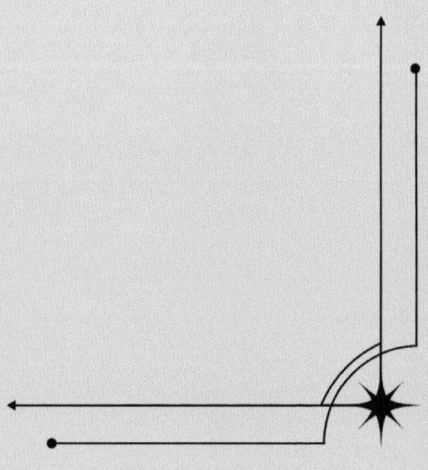

*from the bottom of my heart,
thank You!*

Printed in Great Britain
by Amazon